THE YELLOW WHEELBARROW

POETRY

Plausible Fictions
The Narrators
Get Real!
Acapulco
Of earth, water, air and fire
The Secrets of the Sea
Trench Feet
The Migrant Ship
A Dog's Brexit
The Museum of Truth

FICTION

A Short Book About Love
Remembering Carmen

NON-FICTION

Bruce Chatwin
A Life of Matthew Arnold
After Arnold: Culture and Accessibility
World Enough and Time: The Life of Andrew Marvell
Aldous Huxley: An English Intellectual
Kafka
A Corkscrew is Most Useful
So Spirited a Town: Visions and Versions of Liverpool
Real Bloomsbury
The Red Sweet Wine of Youth: British Poets
of the First World War
Bloomsbury and the Poets
Crossings: a Journey through Borders

THE
YELLOW
WHEELBARROW

Nicholas Murray

THE MELOS PRESS

First published in 2019 by
The Melos Press
38 Palewell Park
London SW14 8JG

ACKNOWLEDGEMENTS

Acknowledgements are due to the periodicals in which
some of these poems first appeared: *Dark Horse*,
Mechanics' Institute Review, *New Boots and Pantisocracies*,
New Walk, *Scintilla*, *Spectator*, and *Tablet*.
'Walk' was winner of the Basil Bunting Award in 2015.

ISBN 978-0-9955173-2-5

Printed and bound in Great Britain by
The Dorset Press, Dorchester DT1 1HD

To S.

CONTENTS

JIGGER

An Appointment With The Devil

He kept coming round, each time in a new disguise:
those famous horns capped in a daft beanie
on which was embroidered (red on black) *Bad Boy!*

Once, as a carpenter, nicely pleased with himself,
stroking with podgy hands the grain of a new sill;
another time as plumber, hunting a sly leak in the loft.

She stood at the ladder's foot handing up a torch.
Now the dog can see the rabbit! said the voice above the legs
as he scrambled in the rafters quietly cursing.

Once as boiler-man, taking out his big spanner
to twist (*heavy breathing*) a recalcitrant brass nut
and curse again the world of the unyielding.

Then the clumsy proposition at the door
that was quickly closed, her back against it:
her breath coming faster than the slam of a bolt.

THE LAMPEDUSA CROSS

Sea-thrown, retrieved
by the island carpenter

who shaped these fragments
of a painted hull

(green-yellow-blue)
into a slender cross

its arms outstretched
to offer comfort

to the wave-washed
driven to the shore

carrying their grief
like a question put

again and again
to the snapping wind.

THE DEAD

This is strange, for I thought that our business was done
when I caught myself climbing up to the porch
where a glossy black car was imperiously parked
and I turned in mid-quip to catch sight of the box
whose varnish and brasses now brought me up short.

I thought you were gone, the tensions and errors
of judgement and speech, that we were both guilty of,
settled and finished, our accounting all done,
all the tackle cleared out from the scatter on deck,
all sorted and shaken and ship-shape and coiled.

This is strange: how you come to remind me of this:
that things are unfinished, that it's madness to think
that nothing at all now remains to be said,
when the opposite palpably beats on the mind
and the heart, and still we must try what we can.

So make the first move, fire the opening gun,
tell me the things that you struggled to say
and intend to resume as we gather our blotters
and fidget our hands on the table's green-leather,
the copier's agenda just falling, clack-clack.

Can we conjure from silence the talk we evaded
and start to sketch out the chat we'd have had?
I'd start but in seconds dry up and then stammer
while you watched with your vigilant, ruminant eye
and out of your silence at last I would get it:

that nothing we say can possibly change
what runs like a river under the stones
where we walk, where silence is natural,
where talking is approximate, and nothing
is something, something to say.

FLOOD

Here is a man,
thinking of a woman,
wanting to bridge
the swift-flowing river
that brings whole trees
from a violent flood
in its turbulent water;
the roof of a house;
an abandoned car;
a terrified horse
screaming its pain.
The woman appears
on the far bank,
in a blue dress,
signalling her love
but he cannot hear her words
which the wind steals
so there is nothing left
but her silence
and her blue dress
and her eyes which say
that she would cross the river
if it could calm itself
after the flood;
that they would bridge
the swift-flowing water; that
they would join
like the two segments
of a sliced pear
someone has parted
with a clean knife.

The Yellow Wheelbarrow

(After William Carlos Williams)

so little depends
on what *I*

think
of the

yellow plastic
wheelbarrow

which has
become

a tank
in which

a blanched
earthworm

fails
to swim.

THE MUSEUM OF TRUTH

They could not tell me where it was
though some had heard its name

so I was left to wander through the streets,
down futile avenues, around locked squares.

I had imagined Doric porticos,
a row of railings capped in gold

but when I found it, on the city's edge,
(in time for 'last admission of the day')

it was a bleak and shuttered barn:
raw concrete streaked by lines of rust.

A bald custodian was at an outside tap,
softening his brittle crust of bread.

He turned with an unpleasant grin
and spat into a nettle-bed.

Inside, the rooms were dusty,
cabinets were draped in sheets,

and on the walls in heavy frames
stiff portraits of the powerful dead.

The prize exhibit was that shining car
they gave the Leader for Inauguration Day.

I imagined shiny tubas, booming drums
beaten by boys in uniform,

high-kicking majorettes
lining that long boulevard

he drove down to the place of power:
the pennants have faded that fluttered then.

He spoke the Truth, they said,
and every word was like a plaque

fixed to a towering wall of fame,
each chiselled letter speaking to the crowds

who later came with tears and flowers
to heap upon his alabaster monument.

OLD LLYWARCH

1

I was the ash with its crown of bright leaf
but the weather destroyed it, forced it aslant.
Lightning unmade it, and savage the grief
that came to reward my arrogant youth.

My songs were renowned in the log-lit long halls
before I was stooped, as you see me, and coughing;
my praise had rebounded from high palace walls;
what my spear had achieved was matter for story.

I am old, I am broken. I am hurt by the seasons.
Autumn's ripeness rebukes me, Winter's iciness stings,
Spring is the worst for the bitterest reasons:
for no love now prepares for the fullness of Summer.

2

In the heartland of Wales, my heart is now dying.
I am hobbled and sick and shunned by the living.
See the stag leap! See the horse's mane flying,
as the daredevils gallop, leaping the hedgerows!

Where are the fields where my banner unfurls?
Where are the hills, unveiling at dawn?
Where did they go, the soft-treading girls
who slipped from my bed in a rustle of silk?

No accident this, no random, chance dealing.
Fate planned it, declared it the price of my living.
My body's dissolving; the world is revealing
each day what I'm bound for: the ruin of Llywarch.

3

Old men are despised for their pantomime weakness:
their stumbling antics, mouths ugly and gaping,
self-hating rebuke, remorse, but not meekness,
for arrogance still breaks out in their insults.

Nothing justifies this, let me warn the unready:
the young and the bold for whom age is a fiction.
You think yourselves certain and your progress so steady,
but my fate shall be yours, and your future as hateful.

THE VOYAGE OUT

Pot-bellied sails, a lively wind, then off.
Our 'loved ones' on the slippery quay,
unsure of what their weeping proves.

After three months, our landfall at Utopia,
the island that imagination made,
the not-a-place that lacks the usual flaws.

That it would fail and break apart
like the scattered carcass of an egg
the stay-at-homes predicted well.

But did they know the whipped breeze,
the first roof raised, the marvellous bird
that carols to us from a jutting bough?

THE MIGRANT SHIP

I

We were too many:
crowded to the rail,
as the quay abandoned us;
water widened.

Don't ask if fear or hope,
drove us in the first days;
don't ask what thoughts
skittered in our heads;

just say we wondered
how long our food would last,
how we might face the heat
of that stinking hold.

II

I spread them on my cloth:
a tiny elephant of brass,
a ring, a ball of glass,
a silver box containing nothing.

III

The boy with the lazy eye
each morning carved a notch
on a stick with a red tassel;
we shunned his tally

having no need
of such knowledge
as the days drifted us
out of reach of time.

IV

Each had his own moment
when the darkness entered
into a personal silence
no one else could share.

I cannot tell you its smell,
bitter taste on the tongue,
the longing to retch
when the stomach is empty.

It was the knowledge of nothing:
that the ship's motion,
which should take us forward,
was infinite regression.

V

I was sleeping when the cries started.
I woke to a panic on the hot deck;
the engines silent and the crew cursing
as the vessel slumped, a sick beast.

One by one we dropped to the water
– boys in a river pool splashing –
but no shore neared,
no watchers called a warning.

Some sank without striving,
others, treading the water,
inspected the ocean,
its taciturn vastness.

VI

When the boats came out
from the sleeping island
they handled us harshly,
shouting in anger

in a strange language.
They hauled us up roughly
over the harsh side,
the ones who were left.

VII

I remember the stillness
as we entered the harbour,
how the gulls cried
from the stone quayside.

I remember the silence,
the fishermen's faces
lifted towards us
as they sorted their catches.

I remember my yearning
for the comfort of sleep
where I hoped to forget
the need for this journey.

I remember the box
that I felt for with fingers
that knew its hinged lid
opened on nothing.

CALAIS

This mud is different.
Were I writing home
I'd struggle to describe
its darker pigment,
how it slips beneath our feet,
a long, slow slide
where boots lose grip.

Under our sheeting
we listen to the rain;
traffic on the near road
lets out a groan, a hiss.
We have learned the art
of slow patience,
of being still, endlessly.

There is always tomorrow,
always the chance
that there will be movement.
Today we cheered
when someone's phone
showed a man walking
out of a tunnel's darkness.

ACROBAT

Now you see me;
now you don't.

That backward flip
that leaves me standing,

and the crowd gasping,
is just for show.

Inside, I'm still;
I haven't moved an inch.

Here on this beach
at the Atlantic coast

fear leaps in my heart,
turns somersault,

in a trick presented
for my private ring.

I am lean and fit
because I rarely eat.

It is not dread of fall
clenches my heart,

Go on, watch this,
as I leap to the shoulder

of my brother
who is not my brother:

the one I abandoned in
the salt dark.

THE UNWRITTEN LOVE POEMS

If they are absent,
or not copious,
I blame the hours
that we have spent;

I mean months and years
lived with no provident
gathering and stacking
of seasoned logs in store

but warming our hands,
wastefully, at the flame
of an improvised blaze
made out of driftwood.

THE QUIZZICOCK

I fabricate a bird,
whose brilliant plumage
foxes the ornithologist,
(the one with a green vest
of many pockets).

He hugs binoculars
to his verdant chest
and whistles slowly
through gapped teeth,
cocks his ear to the sound

my new flyer makes
as it dips from a fir
with a flash of crimson,
blue, white, and gold;
prodigal in its dash,

knowing itself sublime,
too quick to let itself
acquire our admiration.
The quizzicock
crying in the trees,

waiting to be classified,
fitted in, pinned down.
But first a squawk
and upward dart,
glitter of that gold.

KITE

A kite and crow
contest the sky,
like flying aces.

They do not know
the end's foregone,
as in all rigged races.

These feints and swoops,
this mimic violence,
are just a show:

such desperate loops
and air-show tricks,
watched from below,

confirm the strong
at their old game
of hammering the weak.

Though crowds may throng
and bookies thrive,
the victor has the sharpest beak.

MOVEMENT

You pass into another room.
The décor is surprising.

Gone are the cracked plaster,
the broken sash-cord,
the worn carpet and a sofa
whose innards oozed.

Now there are peaches in a glass bowl
on a table-top of veined marble;
a Cornish beach in oils shows an upended
fishing boat, a tump of yellow net.

You unlock yourself.
You let the rush of morning in.

THE TOWER

I met a poet, pointing a barrow of bricks,
the forewheel ploughing a slope.

Why are you pushing this load? I said.
Then, sensing wordplay was expected:

What is the burden of your burden?
Where does the tendered wheel tend?

I am building a house, he said,
a house of stone that a tower will top.

Up this ramp foundations lie
for I know the first thing about how to build:

I shall make my house on firm ground,
unlike this slip and slush where my wheel sticks

on its journey upwards to the site on the cliff
with a glorious view of the bay in all weathers.

(I thought you would like that brochure-touch,
that cocktails-at-dusk round the blue pool.)

Though in fact I am making a trim tower
facing everywhere and nowhere, light-bright.

I will live there and write on blank pages,
the script will crawl like the quick adder

that slips through the long, dry grass,
with arcane knowledge of its destination.

My plan will be simple: to catch my meaning,
(if you catch my meaning) hoping to surprise.

For this is the chimera I chase, the private prey,
the decisive moment when the words pounce

like the lepidopterist's net on fluttering life
that beats its wings for a long moment

before the net is lifted
and the sky reclaims what it lent briefly.

I could talk for hours to avoid writing;
I prefer to build, hauling my red bricks

up this eternal slope where the mud slides and
in winter snow lingers in the deep ruts…

for I am at my best in the light of spring dawn,
the promise of morning a temptation,

when the scratch of my pen
can be heard on dry paper,

as a cloud of starlings noisily swells
above the stilled cypress trees

and somewhere a chapel bell
summons the day to action.

At such times (I like to say) the odour of paradise
seeps slowly into my writing-room…

So, when the tower is done and the slates all fixed;
when the glazing glints and the boards gleam,

I'll be ready to start. Or will there always be diversion?
On days when the carpet-fitters come

with their sharp knives and inimitable banter,
bundling fat rolls from their parked vans,

stripping the green polythene with simian grace,
making obvious comments on the view.

Or the building inspector with her hard hat
and yellow waistcoat, flaps her clipboard

as if it were a signal to distant shipping:
come rescue me from the dark brigand on the clifftop.

There will be gatherings on summer days;
poets and artists, careful of their image,

storing like squirrels the matter of memoir,
making notes on the windy terrace where thyme

puffs its tang and bouquet on that famous wind
that rattles the panes at the end of summer.

There will be days and nights after this is done,
after the last barrow of lime or plaster

stutters like speech to a final stop and stalls
and I watch it, upended, waiting to sink

beneath burying weeds, like a fisherman's smack
his heirs won't care for, letting it rot.

So get out of my light, if I may be so brusque.
I am a poet and have my building to accomplish.

THIEF

Ther cam a privee theef men clepeth Deeth,
That in this contree al the peple sleeth
                Chaucer, *The Pardoner's Tale*

I caught him in the act,
that sly intruder.

No striped jersey
or sack marked SWAG

but a natty designer suit
of soft Italian silk.

He smiled easily,
confident in his strength.

He knew the ropes;
doors opened at a touch.

He had refined his kit
to a leather pouch

crammed with small tools
that could pick a lock

with the pecking swiftness
of a small-beaked bird:

I have what I want,
I would not even say

that I abuse my power
to lift life like a watch

left carelessly on the side,
gold lid wide open,

a stillness in the room
magnified by its tick.

I hardly blinked
and he was gone.

A WEEK OF DREAMS

Monday

She called me to her basement room.
A plate of figs was waiting,
and we talked of our shared love
for the quirky fictions of Georges Perec

until the postman hammered on the door
with a parcel from Guatemala, stamped
exotically and tightly bound with string.
When unwrapped a little book fell free

in which twelve sonnets, each page
bordered by bright blue butterflies,
told a story of love that had failed
because of the indifference of the beloved.

Tuesday

I was running beside a road of furious traffic,
pursued by angry cyclists on noisy gravel.
They tipped me to the harsh thorns of a wild hedge.
Blood popped on my punctured arms and legs.

My plimsolled feet splashed in pools that stank
of some foul substance that I knew was toxic;
my cinder track stretched up to a horizon
that spoke clearly of imminent storm.

Wednesday

On the lake a single sail, a tilted hull
watched from the tall window.
A swarm of bees hurl themselves against
the pane, dropping one by one

as if the game exhausted them,
as if there were no end in view
except extinction, a manic erasure,
their corpses fallen in an amber drift.

Thursday

Here I am, striding out across the square,
towards a raft of ribboned generals
patiently awaiting the salute,
the tanks drawn up, the band prepared

to lift their trumpets, thwack the drums,
and march towards the empty space
that I have left, insurgent, arms outstretched
towards the rifle's urgent crack.

Friday

Darkness, flame in the dark pines
that run towards the sea;
a racing of wolves, teeth bared,
a savage barking.

That is a scream I hear, *ob scena*,
an absent fear that chills me,
vicarious pain, a twisting in the gut,
a distant crying for release.

Saturday

And everywhere bunting, deceitful,
fluttering in the morning sunlight
to celebrate another arrival
whose welcome is a trap,

its jaws closing on the taken bait
before the frightened eyes know
the trick that's played on them,
the laughter on the podium.

Sunday

I woke to a shaft of bright sunlight,
a sky whose clarity was a rebuke
to the vividness of imagining,
to the indulgent running of fear.

I take a glass of fresh juice,
listen to the kettle's music,
catch in my nostrils the shock
of coffee freshly ground.

A Short History of Ethics

Much has been written
on the subject of The Good.
It echoes like a gong

calling us from our sins.
It could be painted
as a bright sun between fronds

of the thrashing sycamore,
a dish of brilliance,
a bright target.

And all around it
what looks like the halo
plaster saints wore

in the dark churches of my youth:
made of tin, tarnished,
but operative as an example.

THE WAY

He came off the mountain in the last of the sun,
leaving the coolness of his summer cave;
winter was breaking, frail ice on the tarns.

We mustered to help but his needs appeared few;
his day was complete with stillness or prayer;
we watched as his smile spread like a stain.

All summer we felt his invisible presence
but when he announced his intention to leave
as the first snows whitened the slopes

we privately uttered a sense of relief.
We couldn't quite take the pressure of Good
that left our small vices nowhere to hide.

Museum Piece

Here is God, with his crucified son
clamped tight between his knees;
on Christ's head sits
the dove of the Spirit
at the level of the Father's groin.

In this way the sculptor
bodied forth the Trinity,
which, as a child in a class
of small, scraped chairs,
I struggled to make sense of.

God the Father, God the Son,
and God the Holy Ghost.

I liked the Spirit best,
thinking birds free to pass
silently through the air:
no sound reaching us
from the far-off beat of wings.

DON'T

It's a rope bridge
whose planks are swaying

The wind counsels:
don't do it, hold to the solid land.

Get a grip on silence, whatever
you say, say nothing.

But whoever listened to good advice?
So we mount the rocking stairway,

the shaken carpet of weathered slats
that lurch and slap then tumble us

through chill, ungracious air
into the deep ravine.

THE EMPTY BOOK

An Empty Book is like an Infant's Soul, in which any thing may be
Written. It is Capable of all Things, but containeth Nothing.
I have a Mind to fill this with Profitable Wonders.
                                                Thomas Traherne

It is a white space
where any act of love
may be performed;

whose primped pillows,
and starched sheets,
wait to be disordered.

Here is spoor of print,
marks that tell
of something live

that has crossed the
empty space,
leaving its trace

like the thin coil
of the sand-worm
on a hard beach

as waves recede
disinclined to wipe
the fresh inscription.

Venus

The painting by Lucas Cranach the Elder, 1531

A girl of Saxony, I'd guess,
disposed by Northern weather
to avoid these naked shows,

persuaded by the painter
to undress inside a room
where ice made dragons

on the window-pane
and lust froze up before the twist
of water left the opened tap.

WE MUST AVOID CLICHÉ

Colleagues, we are ignoring the elephant in the room!
The Head of Marketing is holding her nose,
(painted fingernails a scarlet clamp).
The furrowed hide heaves, ears ripple,
and that wild trunk
sweeps the teacups to the floor.

Your safety is our primary concern.
(and profit, and the pleasure of dominion,
as we watch you crawl along the aisle
whimpering like a beaten dog).

We must reject one-size-fits-all-solutions.
Come to the long room where bald men,
tape measures round their necks like stoles,
dart at your crotch with a knuckle of chalk.

Heart-stopping: brain-stopping.

This long-awaited first collection.
Long-touted on Twitter by its friends,
its enemies not yet found, still to stir
from their long sleep of indifference.

Give us our country back!
It was here a moment ago, I swear.
The empty cupboard had something in it
but I no longer remember what it was.

There is an old Chinese proverb:
May you live in interesting times.

Colleagues, we are living in interesting times.
(That man in the fourth row, his mouth a cavern
open to the salt winds, his eyes closed
in the condition of the fortunate dead.)

JUSTIFIED POEM

It's how we might like it: the end resembling the beginning
neat at both ends and the starting out ending so handsomely,
trim and solid, a block of raw text that signals its substance
with none of the ragged, unkempt sprawl of the unjustified.
It's how we might like it for ourselves, in life I mean to say,
not quite the same thing as centring a vase or flower tub
but starting well and ending in the same fashion: promise of
symmetry, the dark lift of a monument of tall, black marble
whose carved gilt letters memorialise some ancient heroine
and pronounce, in Augustan periods, the honourable life span
in extravagant terms that a later age finds far too mellifluous:
but in the end it won't work for each life must be all random
and formless, and know each minute on the brink of disorder.

WALK

En quoi un homard est-il plus ridicule qu'un chien, qu'un chat, qu'une gazelle, qu'un lion ou toute autre bête dont on se fait suivre? J'ai le goût des homards, qui sont tranquilles, sérieux, savent les secrets de la mer, n'aboient pas... Gerard de Nerval, quoted in Théophile Gautier, *Portraits et Souvenirs Littéraires.*

I see de Nerval coaxing his lobster,
on a leash of blue ribbon.
He has made his case
for preference of pet:
because it does not bark
and knows the secrets of the sea.

In this morning's market
the great crustaceans twitch;
a pair of claws squeezes the air;
liquid eels in slippery ranks
slither on stainless steel;
a salmon sleeps in a drift of ice.

Those bloody aprons,
that pink tump of guts
coiled like a frivolous dessert,
enforce a preference for
the *Bois* – poet and *homard*,
like a pair of lovers, hand in hand.

WHALING MUSEUM, PICO ISLAND

It's just us, in this whip of wind and water:
December in the Azores, blown
from the jetty where they would haul them in.

We seek for refuge among the vats
that melted the hacked blubber.
Crude, long-handled blades

now lean against the walls, unemployed
but visible on the flickering loop of film,
– the hunters running

like part-time firemen from their fields,
triggered by the alarm, the whale spouting,
giving itself away, the light boats racing.

Then bones ground to flour, sperm oil tapped,
everything chopped and fired and milled,
not a sliver or chip, not a tooth of it wasted.

Annotations of Byzantium

1

I am woman and you call me names:
circus dancer, whore, magician...Empress.

Beneath my chamber, secret tunnels run
where men are shut to waste or die;

where night dissolves in day like powders
losing presence in a lethal glass.

They wander in the dark, go mad, lose sight;
I tether them like cattle to a manger

where they feed, a rope around the neck,
who thought they could resist my power.

This I do for Antonina, consort of Belisarius,
the man who cowers while she slakes her lust

with Theodosius, the Thracian boy;
I am woman; I know need and strength.

2

Beneath the dome of Wisdom,
coming from shadows, we greet the patriarch.

Look at our work, great canopy of stone,
mathematics of magnificence.

Later, the salt sea whips my cheeks;
the wind streaks madly from the Dardanelles,

nature and art in passionate contention
where I award, between them both, the prize.

3

He is in the marshes, hunting crane,
watching the violent beat of wings,

patient to cripple the great, beautiful bird
that rises in the mellow light of dawn.

4

They shall say that Theodora rose
'from humble origin', lap-dancer

in the royal eye, to take the purple;
add in 'whore', for it's desire

that frightens them, the narrowed eye,
the jewelled goblet raised and aimed,

a rustle in the chamber's passage
a curtain billows, candle flame

trembles excitedly at what it sees;
lips sealed by willing servitude.

Historical Note

The principal source of this poem is The Secret History *by Procopius (translated, as a Penguin Classic, by G.A.Williamson, in 1966.Written around AD 550 it is a remarkably candid account of the reign of the Byzantine Emperor Justinian and his wife Empress Theodora, who is the narrative voice in the poem.The most famous of the Byzantine emperors, Justinian assumed power in 518 and married Theodora in 523. She died in 547 and Justinian in 565. Justinian is seen as a great law-giver and the period of his reign saw the construction of the basilica of Agia Sophia ('Holy Wisdom') completed in 537 but Procopius tells a story of vicious corruption and tyranny,greed and lust behind the scenes. He also recounts the story of the general, Belisarius, whose secretary Procopius had been, and of his wife, Antonina, who it appears was as corrupt as Theodora herself.*

ISLAND

Brendan's monks have lit a fire
where gutted fish brown on whittled sticks,
and God is thanked for the air of a small island.

There is no hint of what's to come:
the slide of embers, the tilt and scatter,
when the whale lifts itself from seeming sleep.

The Secrets of the Sea

A great shoal of underwater photographers,
trailing plumes of bubbles, track
the ghostly path of sharks, catch
the striped magnificence of fish.

A wristwatch tapped, a clumsy mime
to distant colleagues in their masks;
a finger points into the gloom:
a ray flaps its ancient cloak,

the small fry scatter, and the wrasse's eye
turns in slow disgust
on the limber frog men with false feet.
They work at cataloguing marvels:

what finally evades them is the secret life
of the observed, the enigmatic eye
that watches men, ungainly in the deep,
struggle behind their walls of glass.

INNOCENCE

I shot at a great Bird which I saw sitting upon a Tree on the Side of a great Wood, I believe it was the first Gun that had been fir'd there since the Creation of the World.

Defoe, *Robinson Crusoe*

With the echo of that shot,
the upward beat of wings,
something stained the silence
that could not be scrubbed out.

The man in a shaggy cap
and a patchwork of animal skins
shot off through the undergrowth,
muttering to his beard:

My priority cannot be undone
nor my knowledge of musket and ball,
the cask of dry powder, pistols,
the toolkit of death.

What can I do with such knowledge?
Like liquor spilled on the sand
from the stoppered flask,
I watch it trickle and stain.

After this the footprint,
the certainty of Others,
the slow unspooling
and the not going back.

Too late for regrets:
the sprung Jack has leapt
from the opened box;
the genie has slipped from the bottle.

CUSHIONS

I think of Hans Christian Andersen,
and that troll's feast inside the mountain.

The glittering, illusory people
sitting on dark, luxurious cushions

which were revealed as black mice,
nibbling at each other's tails.

I think of it, watching the voles,
scurrying into the cracks

of a stone wall, so fleet, and light
upon the earth.

THE TROUBLE WITH EPITAPHS

They work through chiselled cold,
when warmth of life, moist breath,
are what I'd like to see epitomised.

I'd have the mason cut a keener font
to catch the lovely sharpness
of a dung-spread field in March;

the bright gleam on an empty road
after a fierce, short drench of rain;
bright air where mild hills interlock.

Inscribe a text for me that lives,
not in this mossy epitaph I trace
with a finger's darkening tip.

JIGGER

THE LAST BUS HOME

On Stanley Road, the turfed-out drinkers,
all their bevvies ended; white-shirted bellies

puffed sails, billowing at the street's corner.
They are going home – but not just yet.

There's blathering in the night air
outside a dozen corner pubs.

Those white bellies luminous moths
in the dark night of the city.

The Curve

First witness of transgression,
watching the men with sideburns

leap to the rear platform of the bus
in its long curve to the Pier Head,

across the wide piazza: the fine swagger
as they leap off, ticketless, insouciant,

steady on their feet like mariners
holding their balance on a plunging deck.

Zero Hours

A stand of men in belted macs,
flat caps, black boots.
See them as trees, black and green,
their mossed trunks glistening.

This man with fingers cut
and bruised from work
probes silently to fix
a broken mower on the lawn;

tells the young boy
what he should know:
when men leapt on
each other's backs

to catch the foreman's eye,
begging for the *sou* of work.
'Get down, men,' he says.
'Where's yer dignity?'

A cough, a straightened back,
a finger wiped across the nose:
'I'm as 'umble as a beggar
burra've got me dignity.'

JIGGER

We ran down the jigger. Past paint-peeled doors
that closed each tiny yard behind the back-to-backs,
we kicked and scarpered, but nothing happened:
no bugger in shirt sleeves came out shouting;
no prune-faced dog offered us its teeth;
no shrill voice screamed; no threats, no chase,
no scuffer bashing his boots on the flags.
What's mischief for, if no one notices?

Later, such light transgressions yielded
to the more painful, practised wrongs

it is our triumph to excel at.

PATINA

After the night-storm, out on the river,
we woke to splashes on the window pane,

light spattering of ochre sand
new rain would wipe away.

Down on the lawn, fragments of leaf,
a plant askew, a clay pot upended.

The day shown through a new lens
wiped with a soft, silk cloth.

THE BACK OF MY HAND

Look here: the private map
no expert could read better.

The faint white scar
a farm fork gashed

on a midden in South West Lancashire:
first job, first blood.

More jobs to come, shuffling paper
into patterns of absurdity,

wasting the hours, the weeks,
in gainful employment,

pacing dreams against the clock,
the slow sweep of its slender hand.

SMALLHOLDING

The *banlieue* is losing its grip.
The suburbs gather to a question:
can we survive the encounter with cold fields
and their rows of turnip and beet, turned by
the silver blades of a plough, a flutter
of shrieking gulls rising above the earth?

Loose dogs of the savage kind
throw themselves against wire, howling
for our blood as we trespass harmlessly
across derelict land, daring each other on,
or digging for the remnants of old clay pipes
near a sweet shop, tiny and fragile as a shed.

Cinders and amateur landfill,
abandoned junk, a spewing mattress,
corrugated iron and everything malformed
and jagged and unlovely stacks itself
and is wrapped in the tendrils of bindweed,
white trumpets of convolvulus.

A place that through the years has receded,
my grip on it tenuous, memory
working now to retrieve it, a mad machine,
pumping and wheezing, blowing steam;
its clanking parts rattle and shake,
but only straws on an empty belt emerge.

Rooted

It might happen here: on a beach of hard sand
studded with niggardly shells, fringed with wrack:

Memory strains to recapture
its point of departure, the first scurrying steps,

that have ended here, on a winter's morning,
sunlight on the smooth surface, a scatter of tracks

where the seabirds run in eccentric circles,
just able to withstand buffets of wind.

It might happen here that something is grasped
that cannot, at last, be relinquished.

The silent child at the upper window
watching the coasters' ponderous progress

on a grey sea, under a grey sky, frozen
in endless afternoon boredom.

Somewhere a siren cries out
its strident warning to the day.

It might happen here that a deal is done
with greedy creditors; the nib scratches

a compliant signing, a willingness to yield
to the insistence of belonging

to this place. The wind chases light sand
along the flat beach, driftwood lies

at casual angles and the walkers of dogs
strain their eyes to the shore, to the sea.

It might happen. It might happen. Here.

THE BOY

Look! Look now
at his blackened feet,
running, running

on the round cobbles
of the long street
that dips to the river,

only to meet
the massive walls
of an unseen dock.

Give that boy shoes,
give him striped socks,
give him leather laces

drawn in a tight bow.

THREE BROTHERS

Christmas morning.
Coming across the lawn,
three short men in Sunday suits.

Try it again
with four sisters:
uncles and aunts,

bearers of gifts
to the children who watch
from an upper window

already tearing the starred
and reindeered paper off.

HERE

Here is a man whose mind has gone,
who drops from an upper window
to the soft, accommodating earth.

Here is the squad-car pausing
on the smooth camber of the asphalt road,
lifting him gently in the mild midnight.

Here is the high hospital tower,
its lights all glaring, its moat of cars:
open all hours, a store of convenience.

Here is the white, high-sided cot
where with my mother I contend
to tug the sheet that shields his modesty.

Here is the innocence of a child.
Here is the fierce, bright light in his eye.
Here is my father, dying.

MNEMONIC

I lift the brass bell:
a woman in full skirt,
in whose folds
black stain lingers
after my diligent steel wool
has scoured time's tarnish.

Holding her head
between finger and thumb,
letting her swing,
I hear a sweet tinkle
under her skirts,
but who am I calling?

From my mother I accept
this not-quite-heirloom,
for she has moved away
from the burden of things
having no need, in her late days,
for the clutter and echo of stuff.

AFTERWARDS

Afterwards, when he had 'gone'
she walked to where the car was parked.

It was that coat of ice,
glueing the wipers to the screen,

that did it, broke the seal,
and let it out.

Give 'it' what name you like,
the frozen ground

made the tears flow
as in legend from a struck rock.

WODGE

I'd like to think it was our tongues
(recalcitrant, not coldly mocking)
that made the new boy into "Wodge".
The best that we could do.

So Wodziński, the doctor's son,
shared my double-desk
and when his lid was lifted
the mess was mesmerising.

This was primal chaos:
torn jotters, chocolate wrappers,
broken pencils, various kinds
and orders of abandoned food.

I think of him now as a surgeon,
bow-tied, sleek, a gracious manner
towards the parents of the child
whose tumour he has neatly taken out.

PARBOLD

In a Lancashire church you left your hat,
its abandonment transformed into a legend.

Why did you not go back? Why did it sit
for ever on a polished bench, unclaimed?

What kind of hat was it? One of your pork-pies
of green tweed with that central crease or fissure?

Or a more stylish trilby, a little forties,
a little *noir*, like the titfer of a private dick

walking the night in his long coat (to strident music)
while the villain gave it wellie in a finned car?

We will be like you, leaving stories behind,
half-finished, puzzling, with no point.

Proverbs Subverted

Too few cooks spoil the broth:
give me a crowd, stomachs pressed against the copper,
stirring vigorously with their great wooden spoons.

Two birds in the hand are worth one in the bush.
Trussed for the oven, their plump sizzle and crackle
drowning the sound of that solitary chirp in the myrtle hedge.

Rarely a slip between cup and lip:
the first instinct right and true,
the brimful glass lifted smartly and swallowed.

Don't look before you leap
lest the view from the tor, dizzying and steep,
crumples resolve, liberates a thousand doubts.

Better never than late: the moment lost,
the word stillborn, the smile dying
when once it lived.

Beggars are choosers; their freedoms flower
in a space of their own making: unsalaried,
untenured, free as the loping, long-eared hare.

Bite the hand that feeds you: relish the sharp *Miaou!*
of the fatcat, nursing his bleeding paw.
That will teach the bastard!

There's no time like the past,
before the wobbling wheel met the precipice,
before a cry ricocheted from the loose scree.

A Premature Request

Without wishing to be prescriptive
in the matter of main course or starter
please put out a plate
of my favourite black olives of Kalamata.

As for what not to do: black ties, long faces,
the obvious signs of grieving
— you should think of it as a party
after someone's leaving.

Keep speeches short and the wine flowing,
for an empty glass is a vile offence
and what is a party but corks popping
and everything in the present tense.

NOTES

Page 10 – 'The Lampedusa Cross' This 40 cm high cross was made from fragments of a boat wrecked in October 2013. The boat was carrying more than 500 refugees and migrants from Africa to Europe. The cross was created by Francesco Tuccio, a carpenter on the island of Lampedusa, as a memorial to the 361 men, women and children who perished in the wreck. It is now on public display in the British Museum.

Page 13 – 'Flood' is partly inspired by a sequence in Theo Angelopoulos' film *The Suspended Step of the Stork* in which a sequence shows the wedding of a young couple while they remain separated by a river marking the border between Greece and Albania.

Page 17 – 'Old Llywarch' was suggested by a translation into English prose of the Welsh poem 'Llywarch Hen' in *A Celtic Miscellany*, edited by Kenneth Jackson and published by Penguin Books.

Page 48 – 'The Walk'. A translation of the epigraph: *In what way is a lobster any more ridiculous than a dog, a cat, a gazelle, a lion or any other animal that one might take for a walk? I am very fond of lobsters. They are calm, serious, know the secrets of the sea, and they don't bark...*

Page 64 – 'Jigger' was published as one of 50 poems in the collective *Poem of the North* (Northern Poetry Library, 2018): it is the Liverpool word for an entry or alley between back-to-back houses. A 'scuffer' is a policeman.